SHIFT!
Change Your Mind, Change Your Walk

Jarixon "Jaro" Medina

Foreword By Dr. Wilfredo (Choco) De Jesus

Shift! Change Your Mind, Change Your Walk
Published by Lindley Books
7711-23 S. Kedzie
Chicago, IL 60652
www.lindleybooks.com

ISBN: 978-1-7353319-5-9 - *Paperback*
ISBN: 978-1-7353319-5-9 - *eBook*

20 21 22 23 24 — 9 8 7 6 5 4 3 2 1

Printed in the United States of America

Endorsements

Jarixon Medina is a dedicated servant of God, a husband, son, father, and now author. I can say this book offers a no nonsense, straightforward approach in assisting the reader on how to overcome negative thoughts that hinder success, growth and spiritual maturity. Not only is pastor Jaro (as he is affectionately called) anointed and appointed by God to preach and speak to the multitudes, I believe he will be used by God to evangelize to thousands that are yearning for revival.

Pastor Efraín Muñoz
Senior Pastor of New Life Covenant Church

Pastor Jaro Medina is a Pastor of New Life Covenant Church a Multi Campus ministry who's impact for the Gospel spans the world. Pastor Jaro in this book "Change your mind, Change your walk" has managed to speak into the spaces and places that have for too long led to dead dreams and dry deserts. This book will give you the courage to dream again, the tools to develop those dreams into reality and not just battle but battle and win over negative thoughts, insecurity, fear, condemnation, and discouragement.

Weaving in personal stories, inspiring examples, and practical strategies, Pastor Jaro through this book and the Work of the Holy Spirit speaks into the valley of our dry bones and calls on us to live again for the Glory of God and to the Glory of God. Excited for how this book will impact the lives of so many.

Rev. Davie Hernandez
Lead Pastor Restoration City Church Ministries "A Multi-Campus Church"

Jaro Medina is an up coming world shaker. The insights that are penned in his book Change Your Mind, Change Your Walk, are the results of his life experiences and challenges as a believer and minister.

Jaro Medina shares with us these divine instructions that will help us avoid the pit falls of unhealthy thought patterns and help us develop a Christ like mind.

Change Your Mind, Change Your Walk is more than just another "must have" book on your book shelf. This is a MUST LIVE everyday book.

JR Rodriguez
Lead Pastor/ Vida City Church Houston

Dedication

I dedicate this book to my wife of thirteen years, Lizette. You have consistently supported me and inspired me to go after my dreams. Thank you for being the kind, strong and wise woman of God that you are. You have shown me so much love and taught me that when you love someone, you always forgive them.

Thank you babe; I couldn't have done this without you. If I had to start life all over again, I would search the entire world until I found you. I love you, my love.

— **Your Negrito Lindo**

Table Of Contents

Foreword

I have had the privilege of pastoring Pastor Jaro, and I have seen growth in his life, family, and ministry here in Chicago. As a lead pastor, I always wanted to be in the expressway of life with individuals who are progressively pursuing destiny. The last seven years, I have seen the shifting in Jaro's life that you are about to read in his book.

I have often said that it is easy for God to move a vehicle already in motion. A parked car doesn't need a GPS; however, shifting means it is moving. I think about the times I've driven cars that utilize stick shift; you constantly need to shift gears. The car lets you know when it's time to shift or change gears. When the vehicle accelerates speed and gets to the 5th gear, you can continue accelerating without making any more shifts. Pastor Jaro's book is about changing or shifting gears to arrive at your destination.

The chapters in this book are all about shifting and arriving.

In his new book, Jaro explores nine different strategies that will help you navigate shifts in practical and spiritual ways. Be prepared because when you get to Chapter 8 of this book, you will be ready to go and prepared to move forward. Shift is a must-read book for those who desire to get to the next level spiritually and practically.

Every chapter of this book will hold deep encouragement and be a blessing to its readers. I look forward to seeing what God will do with and through this book. More than this book is the message. I want to congratulate Pastor Jaro for this great accomplishment and allow his experiences to be written down on these pages. Lastly, if you are experiencing momentum in your life and feel that you are in 5th gear, you need to continue driving and wait until God calls you to decrease your speed. Take your shift and accelerate.

Dr. Wilfredo (Choco) De Jesús

General Treasurer of the Assemblies of God USA

Former Senior Pastor of New Life Covenant Church

Named by Times Magazine (2013) one of the 100 Most Influential People of the World

Introduction

For the past five years, my church, New Life Covenant, has hosted "Safety in the Sanctuary," an outreach event led by our Humboldt Park Campus pastor, David Marrero. In 2016 New Life's former senior pastor, who is now our bishop, Wilfredo (Choco) de Jesús, opened the church to provide shelter to the homeless in our community. This service is completely funded by the church and we usually offer it during the coldest season of the year, allowing people to stay with us for up to twenty-one days. Chicago is commonly referred to as "The Windy City," and during the winter, with wind chills the temperature can drop to negative thirty degrees. In addition to providing shelter, we prepare meals and clothing, and bring in barbers and hair stylists from the church to gift the people we serve with makeovers. At the end of their stay, some who battle with drug addiction decide to make a complete change, and agree to enter into a detox program.

At the beginning of 2020, just a couple of months before the coronavirus pandemic started, I was in the lobby of the Humboldt Park Campus assisting with Safety in the Sanctuary. I started talking to a barber who had come in with one of the church members to drop off food. I learned that although he wasn't a member of our church, he'd come with his barber equipment and decided to help. Was this a coincidence? No, it was divine intervention. This man had shown up on purpose.

As he worked, we talked; he started by telling me how he got to the church that day. We were having a great conversation and I could tell that he was a good man. Eventually he began to share some of his life experiences. He told me how he'd spent most of his youth and adult years in and out of prison, but he was determined and able to turn things around to create a better life. I began to encourage him about the changes and good decisions he'd made. I shared that it's never too late to head in the right direction.

This conversation was like many that I'd had before. I enjoy encouraging people, especially men who are turning their lives around and making good choices. But the talk I was having with this young man led me in a direction that I didn't expect. It ended up birthing something in my life that I had no idea was inside of me. The barber looked at me and at Pastor Josh, who had joined in our conversation. Softly and sincerely he said, "Pastor, thank you. I have changed, but the only things that I can't overcome are smoking weed and lust for women." He looked down in defeat.

I placed my hand on his shoulder and he lifted his eyes to meet mine. I replied affirmatively and firmly, "Changing your life doesn't happen by changing your actions. Change happens by changing your *mind*. There has to be a Shift. If you change your mind, you will change your walk."

After those words left my lips, I was immediately aware that I'd said somthing significant. I felt that power had just been released. I glanced over at Pastor Josh and his eyes looked at me questioningly, as if to say, *what did you just say?* That's when it hit me. *That should be a book,* I said to myself. *Shift, Change Your Mind, Change Your Walk.*

Since that day in the church lobby with that incredible young barber, I have been thinking about the idea of the shifts that needs to happen in order to change our minds and change our walk. When I use the term "walk" I mean the direction in which we end up traveling in our lives.

If you've ever driven a manual car, you will know that in order for the car to go faster and further, there must be a SHIFT. If you don't shift gears you will burn the engine. In life is the same, there must be a shift in the mind in order to experience a change. But for some odd reason many people will try to go faster and further without making the necesarry shifts in their mind to experience the changes they desire, and as result we have many people burnt out not wanting to go faster nor further. Simply, just stuck.

As I explored this further, I began researching and reading related books. Eventually I started to write, and the result is the book that you hold in your hands.

I believe this content can help anyone who wants to experience something new in their life, to change their minds. I hope to give you nine important shifts to lead you to change your lifestyle, reach your goals, start a new business, or overcome addiction. The first step towards change is not dependent on your actions or habits, though they are important. You have to begin with your mindset.

I pray that as you read this book something will begin to stir within you that will lead you to birth a new thing. I believe you will find inspiration and courage to shift your thinking. I pray that you will experience true change and a turnaround in your life. It is my hope that you will pass along what you learn from this book to peers, business partners and even the next generation. I believe that because you decided to *Shift,* this will *Change Your Mind* and *Change Your Walk,* in such a way that you will leave a legacy of transformed men and women, who think and act differently. Enjoy!

Special Instructions

There are several ways to read this book. You can read it on your own or in a group. If you are reading independently, I encourage you to read a chapter per week, even though you can probably read this entire book in one week alone. I suggest taking your time. You may find yourself reading and re-reading chapters, which is fine. The more that the content saturates your mind, the more likely you will apply what you have learned. Take notes on the things that you have applied and write down your results. Make sure to review the questions at the end of each chapter and take time to think about your answers. Some chapters may take you longer to review. That is okay, go at your pace.

Do not get discouraged if you do not see changes take place right away. The important thing is to make sure you are applying what you've learned. Remember, knowledge without practice is just knowledge. But if you put it into practice, you will see its power. At the end of the week you should reflect on what has worked for you. Make note of what you find, and continue to apply it until your learnings become part of your life.

If you're reading this book as part of a group, you can apply the same principles. Read and review one chapter per week, and apply what you have learned. The difference here is that you will want to discuss the chapter with the group when you meet. For example, if your team meets on Mondays, you should start the book on the Monday before. When you meet, everyone can discuss their personal experiences about the chapter. It is very important that there is not any judgement passed. You may notice that some chapters are more difficult for some people to process, and that's okay. This will be a journey of growth and appreciation. I guarantee that at the end of the study, your group will be stronger and more united.

SHIFT 1

Detox Your Mind

You may have heard that detoxing at least once a year is helpful for your body. Detox cleanses are recommended to prevent diseases that can develop in the colon. Although some healthcare practitioners don't believe it is necessary, others strongly recommend it. Personally, I think it can be benefical to not only your physical body, but to your mind, too. Detoxing is necessary to get rid of our old ways of thinking. To change the way you walk out your life, you have to start with the way that you think. For many people that is harder to accomplish than it sounds, especially if the way that they think was shaped by their childhood. Changing may require dismantling years or even decades of believing and living based on a wrong mindset.

There can be many reasons why a person has a negative way of thinking. It could be the result of a bad experience such as betrayal by a trusted person or career failure. Your view of these types of situations can create a wrong mindset, which influences your thinking. This will affect your ability to trust people, your personal development, relationships and overall success in life. Your level of dedication and the attitude you take towards establishing your goals begin with your thoughts.

The way that you think also can be greatly influenced by the way that you were raised. Many experts in psychology and the study of human behavior support the idea that a person's upbringing and their childhood surroundings will influence the way he or she thinks. Let's say that you grew up in a family where everyone has a tendency to be negative. They don't believe anything that cannot be proven. They are realists; they only trust what they can perceive with their senses. These family members do not allow themselves to imagine. They are not dreamers. In fact, they view it as a waste of time. Over the years, you may have heard things like, "be real," "stop dreaming," "get your head out of the clouds," "those people inherited money from their parents," or, my favorite, "you need money for that and we don't have it."

If you can relate, lean in a little closer, I'd like to share something with you. But first, let me make sure I'm talking to the right people. Are you tired of hearing that "you can't" do something? Is there something inside of you saying that things shouldn't have to stay the same? Do you have clear goals and dreams, but no one to support you? If you answered yes to any of these questions, I have some good news. You don't have to continue experiencing the same things. You can do the very thing you desire, your circumstances can change, and you can pursue your goals and dreams. How? By deciding to detox and change your mind, and thereby, the way that you think. That same, old, negative way of thinking got you to where you are now. What makes you think that continuing with this way of thinking can take you to a better place? The truth is, it can't. You have to choose to be different—you have to make a change.

Costs of Not Changing Your Mind

The reality is that your current way of thinking is costing you. Maybe you've passed up business opportunities that others took on. Now they are living their dreams while you seem to be stuck in the same place. You may even dislike those people because it feels like they took something from you. But that's not true. No one took anything from you. The truth is you simply didn't jump at the opportunity and you missed out. You allowed the way that you think to paralyze you.

Paralysis is a condition of the mind.

Paralysis is a physical condition for some, but for others it is a condition of the mind. It is caused by overthinking—the kind of thinking that makes people focus on every detail to the point that they become overwhelmed and don't dare go after an opportunity. Overthinkers analyze everything, but accomplish nothing; this is what produces paralysis. This has happened to all of us at one point or another. We've found ourselves in situations that we were unsure about, and we overanalyzed the issues. Before we realized it we found a way to talk ourselves out of pursuing an amazing opportunity.

This mentality has to change. Your old way of thinking has already cost you too much. It has kept you from pursuing your dreams. It has made you content with living at the status quo, and unable to see beyond your current living conditions. It has prevented you from providing the lifestyle you want for your family, and held you back from being bold and changing the way you're living. Your old, negative mindset hasn't allowed you to step into the light and finally become the person God created you to be. Instead, you have to be fake in front of people because you want to be a pleaser, and be liked by everyone. You've settled into being unhappy, and behaving like a person that you are not. You and I both know that you are probably well past the threshold of being tired. You're done.

My Radical Mind Change

I remember when I got to the point when I was done living this way. I was unhappy with what I was doing. I was unable to provide the life I wanted for my family, and at one point I had to live on government assistance. To be clear, there is nothing wrong with that. We all need help at one time or another and this doesn't make you less of a person. So, there was a time when I had to use food stamps to buy groceries for my family. At first it was embarrassing, but I know now that was my pride rising up. We needed food stamps, and it was helpful when our daughter was born.

There also was a time when I was unemployed and my daughter needed shots. We didn't have health insurance and I had to go to a clinic that only helped people with lower incomes.

The system there was a mess. It was in the basement of a courthouse. The place was filthy, and by the time I'd gotten there it was packed with people so there was no place to sit. Instead of calling out people's names with courtesy, the workers were yelling at us. I thought to myself, *"Man, if these people are tired of their jobs let someone else take their job."* After my daughter's appointment was finished, I left that place angry. I felt like such a failure. I was living just below poverty level because a "system" decided that's who we were. I told myself that I would never step foot in that place again.

I was unemployed and I got tired of being on unemployment. I'd think about previous supervisors and how they got their jobs. My thoughts were negative, *"just because you're white you think you're better than me,"* or *"who do you know that got you this position?"* That way of thinking didn't allow me to give my best.

Over the years I looked for new jobs, and I began to land position after position, but couldn't keep any of them. We were in the midst of the 2008 recession and jobs were unstable; I'd get a job and then get laid off. I probably went through more than five jobs during that season. At one point I became unemployed for an extended period of time. There was nothing that I could've done to prevent being laid off. The last person hired usually had to be the first one let go. I was crushed, angry, and not willing to accept that reality.

Something had to change. While standing in the unemployment line once again, I told myself, *"I am a son of God, I will see great things in my life and I will find a good job."* So I did what

I had never done in all of the times I had visited that office previously. I left my place in line, went home and called my wife at her job. When she answered the phone I said, "Babe, I left the unemployment office."

You can probably imagine that didn't go well. She couldn't believe what I had done. She immediately launched what seemed like a thousand questions at me.

"What are we going to do? What are you going to do? How are we going to provide? My income alone is not enough. What were you thinking? You are being prideful. You need to go back," she said. I listened patiently.

After she was finished I simply told her, "I will find a job. Trust me."

To be honest, my wife almost left me. This isn't something we talk about much, but we were having a conversation in the car and I remember her saying to me, "Jaro, since we've been married you haven't been able to keep a job. I don't know what to do." She was telling the truth. The reason that I could not hold down a job was because of my way of thinking. I didn't like anyone telling me what to do. That was a huge problem, and my preconceived ideas about supervisors made me disrespect them. The amount of respect you give to someone often depends on how you perceive them. For example, if your supervisor is younger than you or does not have the same skin color, you may mistreat them. But being respectful to someone cannot be not based on age or color; everyone deserves to be respected. So, how you treat them says more about you than it does them. It takes maturity to understand that.

Going back to the conversation with my wife, I couldn't respond to her statement—*since we've been married you haven't been able to keep a job.* I knew she was thinking about leaving me, and all I could say to her in that moment was, "Babe, I will respect whatever you want to do."

She began to cry. "I'm not going anywhere," she said. "But please do something about this."

That was all of the motivation I needed. I got busy. I applied for jobs, dressed up for interviews, and made sure that I was on time. All of a sudden I had choices. I looked at what jobs paid better, and which ones had health benefits. It was amazing that I was able to *choose* the best option for me and my family. Within weeks, I had a job that I wanted. From there, I secured better jobs and by 2014 I landed what I call "a career job." I became a service technician for Cummins Allison, one of the largest money counting product and service providers in the U.S. The job came with a good salary and benefits, a company vehicle that was updated every few years, and a gas stipend. I was able to take the car home and use it on the weekends. It was amazing. For the first time I could take my wife out on date night and valet park the car because I wasn't embarrassed about what I was driving. I came to appreciate every life experience that led to that job.

I was not about to mess up this opportunity. I worked hard and always looked professional. My supervisor, Heath Wood, regularly called to tell me what a good job I was doing, because the customers often gave him positive feedback. Many of them told him that they only wanted me to service their machines. Mr. Wood created a great work environment and I was doing well.

22

After a year or so, I applied for a higher position in the company's corporate office—and I got the job! When I got home I told my wife and she couldn't believe it. It was a twenty thousand dollar salary increase. By changing my way of thinking, I was now growing in every area of my life.

The same week I received the new job offer, my pastor called and said that he wanted to talk to me. After a brief discussion, he offered me a pastoral role working for the church. It would require a major pay cut, but I knew that it was my calling. For years, I'd known that at some point I would have to make the decision to go into full time ministry. But I never expected it to happen at the same time that I received an amazing job offer.

I prayed about it and spoke to my wife; we both felt that I needed to accept the role with the church. In my prayer time I said, *"Really God? I've finally got a good job and possibly a great promotion, now is the time that you make a way for ministry?"* Nevertheless, I accepted the pastoral role without hesitation, taking a thirty thousand dollar pay cut. I called the corporate office to decline the job offer, and then met with my supervisor. It was the saddest letter of resignation I'd ever had to turn in. On my last day of work I cleaned my truck. I cried the whole time. It seemed as if I used more of my tears than soap and water to do the cleaning. I loved that truck and I loved my job. My boss told me, "I'm going to hold your position for two years. If things don't go well, you'll have a job with me. But I know you're going to do great." I was thankful that I left such a good impression. As it turned out, I never looked back.

Steps to Detoxing Your Mind

It has been almost eight years since I left the unemployment office frustrated and overwhelmed, and thankfully I have never returned. I have thrived in my role at the church. Our ministry is growing, even in the middle of the novel coronavirus COVID-19 pandemic that we are currently facing. For the first time I have enjoyed lengthy vacations with my family, and even have gone house hunting. We are finally in a position to afford a home, and although we don't have plans to move, just having the option at this point in our lives is mind blowing.

It is incredible to see what can happen when you decide to change your mind. Now that I've shared some of my story as an example of how detoxing my thinking changed my life, I'd like to share how you can do it, too. It may feel as if you need a brain surgery to shift your thinking. Detoxing our thought processes can seem to be impossible, especially if we have been thinking a certain way since we were very young. Thankfully, initiating change is not complicated. Let's look at three steps that you can take to start.

1. Become an enemy of conformism.

   Many people can't find the strength to change because they are comfortable. They have maintained a way of thinking for so long that they believe it is impossible to change. Let me tell you, it is posible, but you have to decide to become an enemy of conformism. Whenever you feel as if life doesn't have any more to give you, that there isn't anything else to accomplish, that you can't break out of your family cycles, you have to make a decision to shift. Shake off those feelings, stand up, hold your head high and say, "Here I come. I refuse to live like this any longer. I will amount to something great." It doesn't matter how much you have already accomplished. You can be a business owner, a multi-millionaire, or a billionaire; know that there is still more. As a pastor, I go to the Bible as the number one source to guide my thoughts and beliefs. Romans 12:2 (NIV) makes it clear, "<u>Do not conform to the pattern</u> of this world, but be transformed by the renewing of your mind." The world's systems want you to be conformed to what you have, and stay where you are. But clearly God doesn't want us to conform to the way this world operates. Instead, His desire is for us to be transformed. How? By renewing our minds.

2. Believe that you deserve better.

   Many people can't make changes in their lives because they don't believe that they are deserving of more. And because they don't realize they deserve better, they don't think you do either. They may say to you, "Hey you've changed," as a way of expressing their displeasure with the new way that you are behaving. Let this be a reminder that you don't have to ask for permission from anyone to change. It is your God-given right to evolve and be prosperous. It is your God-given right to become a better person, achieve your dreams, and become the best version of yourself.

   Your economic status and accomplishments don't necessarily translate to happiness. There are many people that have abundant possessions and riches, and still are not happy. Others are not happy because they have nothing. These people may not pursue happiness because they believe that they don't deserve to be happy or feel accomplished. Let's look at what the Bible says in Ephesians 4:23-24 (NLT) "…<u>let the Spirit renew your thoughts and attitudes</u>. Put on your new nature, created to be like God—truly righteous and holy." Your thoughts and your attitudes need to be renewed. There is a new nature that God has for you, to become like Him. It may seem unbelievable, but it is true. God wants you to change. All you have to do is put on His new nature, which is righteous and holy. Then you will understand that you deserve all of the blessings that come with that. Ephesians 1:3 (NIV) says, "Praise be to the God and Father of our Lord Jesus Christ, who has blessed us in the heavenly realms with every spiritual blessing in Christ." This scripture lets us know that God has blessed us, past tense. We don't need to ask God for what He has already given us. Stop trying to chase something that is already yours. It belongs to you. All you have to do is partner with God to receive it. Ask God to reveal the way He wants you to go about it. During your prayer time, ask Him how your stored up heavenly blessings can be released to you. God may want you to start a business, enter into a new career or create a new invention. It is your responsibility to develop any idea that God gives you. I will address this more in a later chapter.

3. Guard against negative thinking.

   Imagine for a moment that you are standing outside of a night club. There is a security guard at the door checking IDs. His job is to make sure that everyone who enters the facility is of age. If they are not, he will deny that person entry. Your mind works the same way. You need to set guards over your mind, to stay on the lookout for negative thoughts. You need to identify each thought, and those that are not going to benefit your new way of thinking you need to deny entry. In other words, do not allow them in.

   Second Corinthians 10:5 says, "…and we take captive every thought to make it obedient to Christ." Notice the word captive. This is how we must treat every negative thought. And we are supposed to take them captive to the obedience of Christ. Through Christ you have a new nature, and whenever any thoughts go against that nature you must take them captive so that they obey Him. To make this work practically, you need to talk to yourself. I know that sounds crazy, but it works. Listen to what you say to yourself in your mind. Take captive anything negative and train your mind to only accept positive thinking. Replace negativity with thoughts like:

   ♦ There is no room for negativity in my mind.
   ♦ I don't think that way anymore.
   ♦ That's not me.
   ♦ I'm better than that.
   ♦ I refuse to go back to my old way of thinking.

- ♦ I'm a new person, negative thoughts have to go.
- ♦ You're not occupying any space in my mind.

I believe that these statements will greatly help in your transformation process. Replace every negative thought with a positive one, and continue to talk to yourself in that manner.

Now that you know that you have been blessed, you can be assured that you deserve all of the blessings that God has already prepared for you. And you don't have to be apologetic. The blessings are yours because God gave them to you.

Changing the way you think cannot be accomplished overnight. Be patient and don't give up. Take it from me, it will take time. I was the person who overanalyzed everything due to fear.

But once I got tired of allowing my overthinking to paralyze me and keep me from my goals, I began to accomplish everything God put in my hands to do. Each thing that I accomplished brought its own benefits. The benefits of having a new mindset include eliminating the fear of failure, and elevation.

Some people think that your blessing will only come when you pray, fast, and read the Bible. I don't agree with that way of thinking. While those are good things to do, in my case, God's overwhelming blessings didn't come solely because of my spiritual discipline, they have come because of my changed mind. I had to believe God's blessings were for me, and receive them by walking out what I believed. God will open doors for you; He will give you favor with people who will help you. But it is your responsibility to put in the work.

Chapter Review

- ♦ What has led to some of your negative thinking?
- ♦ Being a dreamer has allowed me to achieve...
- ♦ Being a dreamer has caused me hardships such as...
- ♦ What circumstances have led you to a radical mind change?

Think Like a Child,

Walk Like a Man

I'm the proud dad of two beautiful children. My daughter, Jayliz, is ten and my son, Jeremiah, is five. Sometimes I overhear them talking while they're playing; the way they use their imaginations is amazing. My son plays with his wrestling toys and at times he invites Ken from my daughter's Barbie collection to fight. They have the best WrestleMania matches. My daughter plays with her Barbies and My Little Pony toys and she thinks they are actually flying around the room with her. You know, we all were like that at some point. We had great imaginations. We dared to dream without fear, saying, "I will be 'this or that' when I grow up."

But then life happened to us. Along the way we found out that things were not what we thought they were. We began to realize that life was not a dream. We heard our peers or parents say things like, "don't dream too big," "be more realistic," "that will take too much money," or "no one in our family has ever done anything like that."

Never disconnect from your imagination.

A child always wants to have fun. It's been proven that children will learn more if they find learning enjoyable. Adults are always looking for an opportunity to teach children, which is our responsibility. But we can make a big mistake when we take fun out of the equation. We may find out later in life that our children don't want to spend time with us because we won't have fun. In the right environment, learning can and should be fun. We have to realize that keeping a childlike mentality can positively affect the way that we spend time with our children. You can't put a price on that.

The Chess Lesson

One Sunday evening we went to the home of our associate pastor, Victor Santiago, and his wife Carmen, for dinner. They are amazing people and have a beautiful family. At the dinner table we started talking about life. Victor began to share the things he had been learning from his grandkids. He told us that we need to remember to have fun, even while we teach our kids, so they will love spending time with us. This man is full of wisdom. He is seventy years old and he knows that he can learn from anyone, including his grandchildren.

He went on to tell us that a few days prior he was playing chess with one of his grandsons. He said that he went into teaching mode. He was playing him hard, teaching him everything about the moves he needed to make and the importance of each chess piece. Since he wanted his grandson to learn, he was not allowing him to win. After so many games his grandson told him, "Grandpa, can you please let me win one?" Victor's voice cracked as he imitated the soft voice of his grandson; he was almost brought to tears. He said that he felt so bad in that moment. All his grandson wanted to do was to have fun while spending time with his Papa, and there was no fun in losing every match.

During the next game Victor let him win. He said the kid's face lit up. He jumped up, yelling, "I won, I won, I won!" As soon as his father came home he ran up to him and said, "Daddy, daddy, I beat Papa!" Victor's grandchild was impacted so deeply by his decision to incorporate a little fun into their game, I can assure you he will never forget it. He will forever treasure that summer night at the dinner table when he made history by beating his Papa at chess. Now Victor's grandson wants to spend more time with him, and Victor is loving it. Everyone wins. And while it is okay to win, we can't lose sight of what's most important—having fun while winning. If that is not happening you need to understand why.

Sometimes you have to be willing to lose in order to win.

The Power of Imagination

Your imagination is a powerful gift from God. The Bible mentions this in Ephesians 3:20, "God is able to do immeasurably more than all we ask or imagine, according to his power that is at work within us" (author's translation). In other words, God is able to do more than all we ask Him to. He is just waiting for people to believe Him and ask for the big things. We shouldn't be asking for small things; the small things are for us to do. The big things are for God to do.

Paul also uses the word imagine in this verse. God can give you what you imagine, whatever your mind can think. He is just waiting for you to dare to think it. The last part of the verse, "according to his power that is at work within us," reveals something important. God's power is working inside of us. We have the power to imagine anything and work hard for it until we get it. But obtaining what we want starts with maintaining a childlike imagination. We have to move into adulthood, which mean growing in responsibility, increasing in integrity, expanding our ethics, keeping our word, respecting others and all of the things we teach our kids to do. But just because we are maturing in these areas, it doesn't mean that we need to get rid of our childlike imagination. We still need it. It is in our imagination where the power of achievement resides. It lays there, dormant until it is tapped.

Unfortunately, many people won't even get to use ten percent of the power that they have, because their imaginations have been held back due to negative life experiences. Those bad experiences likely produced fear, which stops any dreamer in their tracks if they pay attention to it.

The Fear of…

We all deal with fear at some point in our lives. There are so many things we are afraid of — the fear of failure, the fear of not reaching a goal, the fear of going through another divorce, the fear of not being able to get out of drug addiction or alcoholism. You may say things like, "I can't go through this again," "I can't fail again," "I can't…" Unfortunately, as long as you continue to say "you can't," guess what? You won't succeed. This is the equivalent of declaring yourself a failure before you even start. No team goes into a game saying that they're going to lose, even if they have a low chance of winning. Everyone goes into the game thinking they are going to win.

This is a reason why people don't dare to set goals anymore. They are afraid to fail. They don't want to dream anymore because they think it's not going to happen for them. So, they end up just going through life, not realizing their full potential. But that's not the way your Creator intended for you to live. He placed a power inside you and called it "imagination". Use it! don't be afraid.

In his book, *Move Ahead with Possibility Thinking*, Robert H. Schuller said, "Let your imagination release your imprisoned possibilities." In the book, he recommends five ways to make success-generating imagination work for us.

1. Pick a goal.
2. Imagine a variety of possible ways to reach your goal.
3. Excommunicate fear from your imagination.
4. Imagine yourself getting started.

5. Imagine goals beyond your goals.

In a powerful statement, Schuller sums up the importance of goal-setting, "Not having a goal is more to be feared than not reaching a goal."

Keep Dreaming

Don't lose your ability to dream. As we've established, children don't see impossibility, they dream. For adults, dreaming is supressed because of negative experiences, contrary voices in our heads, and the influence of society. Dreaming doesn't align with the agenda of leaders who want to keep people under control. As long as many people continue to live in poverty, maintain a poor mentality, and depend on government assistance, dreaming is not a choice. If people remain in that place of fear and mediocrity, we can't be of influence. It is time to rise up, be inspired, be the change you want to see and begin to dream again. Don't be afraid. Imagine. Dream. Unleash the power that is within and make it work for you.

The Farm

At the end of every school year a teacher takes his class to a big farm. The farm is beautiful and has horses, cows, pigs and many other animals you'd expect to see. The teacher always loves the reactions of his students when they see the breathtaking entrance to the farm for the first time. There is a gorgeous golden gate, with tall palm trees and flowers planted on both sides. The students' trip started with horseback riding, which allowed them to tour the entire farm and learn about farm life. The students concluded their day by meeting the owner of the farm, who would tell them a story.

Once upon a time, there was a boy who had big dreams. The final project assigned to his class was to draw who they wanted to become. One by one, the students brought drawings to the teacher, and they received passing grades. There were drawings of a police officer, a firefighter, a doctor and so on. But this boy was not afraid to dream big and he drew his huge dream on the paper. When he turned in his drawing, the teacher looked at it, paused and asked,

"What is this?"

"This is my dream," the boy replied.

"This is a beautiful dream," the teacher responded. "But it's not realistic. People in this town don't do such big things. Bring me a more realistic drawing tomorrow."

Dejected, the boy dropped his head, took back his drawing and went back to his desk.

"Remember," the teacher called behind him. "This grade can make you either pass or fail my class."

The boy went home and was devastated. He was crying in his room. His father came in to find out what happened. After the boy explained, he said, "Son if this is your dream, stay with it."

The next morning the boy arrived at school. He went into the classroom, and handed in the same drawing. Disappointed, the teacher looked at the boy and said, "Are you sure you want to turn this in? I'll be forced to give you a D-minus. That's a very bad grade."

"It's ok," the boy said. "You can keep your grade. I'll stay with my dream."

The owner of the farm finished the story by telling the class, "That boy was me, and today you're sitting in my drawing."

The reason this boy was able to one day walk out his dream, was because he put it on paper. Don't give up on your dreams. Write them down, draw them, and make them a reality. Keep your dreams in front of you until they become tangible. Let people keep their opinions—you stay with your dreams.

Chapter Review

- How important is your imagination for your journey?
- How can you recover your child-like imagination?
- Fear has stolen _____ from me.
- What are you willing to do to take back what fear has stolen?

SHIFT 3

Control Your Mind

Your mind is more powerful than you think. If you are able to control your mind, you will eventually control your outcome. Be honest with yourself. Have you ever gone into a meeting in a bad state of mind and the outcome of that meeting was awful? Because you went in with a poor attitude you had a poor experience. That's how powerful your mind is. It can influence your results in life and even your future. If you want to fail in life, just think that you will. The same is true if you want to win. If you think you will win, you will.

The Bible speaks about this in the book of Proverbs 23:7, which says, as a man thinks in his heart, so is he. This scripture is saying that if you find out how you think, you will discover who you really are. The way a person thinks will tell you a lot about them—the way that they process things, the way they say things. When you go out to a restaurant, pay attention to how people treat the waiter. It can show you what they think about people whom they perceive to be beneath them. It can show you who they really are.

The same can be true about yourself. You must find the way to discover how you think. How do you process things? How do you treat those who are at a lower level than you? How do you talk about people? How do you see things play out in your mind? It is so important to find out who and where you are. Why is this so important? Because many folks have gone through life wanting to be someone they see on television, or wanting to be like someone they read about, leaving out who God created them to be. By ignoring God's input they try to become someone that goes against their original, master design.

Better to be patient than powerful;
better to have self-control than to conquer a city.
— *Proverbs 16:32 (NLT)*

I'm not saying that you can't admire others. I personally admire people who have certain traits that I'd like to apply to my life. Examples include Dr. John C. Maxwell, Bishop Wilfredo de Jesús (a.k.a. Pastor Choco), Bishop T. D. Jakes, Pastor John F. Hannah, and Mark Cuban. I admire certain traits about these men; I admire them in areas that they have excelled in. They have mastered certain things and because I know that those areas in their lives can add value to me, I want to imitate and learn from them. But that is very different than wanting to be them. I have to be comfortable in my own skin. I need to accept who I am. But the issue with many people is that they don't know who they are, because they haven't paid attention to the way they think. When you pay attention to how you think, and find out who you are, that will tell you where you are.

Not knowing where you are in life will trump your direction, your future and your vision. You must face the reality of your life. The way that you determine that is to ask yourself where you are at this moment. Are you stuck, exceeding expectations, preparing, moving, leading, living, surviving, or dying without knowing it? By finding out how you think, you can discover if you are in a moment in your life where you need to do some soul searching.

The Trap of Unforgiveness

Often, when we do a real soul search we discover that unforgiveness dwells in our hearts. Something that happened in your past is still lingering. Maybe when you started your business someone did you wrong, and that is still deeply rooted in your heart. Or perhaps in your childhood you were mistreated and you haven't been able to get past it. Whatever the issue, you need to forgive the individual who hurt you. Why am I writing about forgiveness in an inspirational book? It is because many times, a person who is stuck, bitter, not growing could possibly be carrying unforgiveness.

Unforgiveness will occupy space in your mind and heart until you address it. The unforgiveness in your heart shapes the way that you think about others and your future. Remember, as a man thinks in his heart, so is he. You will find yourself not trusting people in your life because unforgiveness dwells in your heart. You will find yourself not allowing new friends or business partners into your life, all because of unforgiveness. By not forgiving, you are allowing toxic feelings from your past to contaminate your goals and dreams. Unforgiveness, bitterness, and hate will not allow you to move forward in life, because they will always keep you connected to your past.

In your soul searching, you might find that you still hold a grudge with someone and you never forgave them. I'm not trying to dismiss what happened to you. As a matter of fact, you may have every right to feel what you do. But giving yourself the right to not forgive is giving unforgiveness the right to rule your life. It will ruin your future. Why? Because as Dr. John C. Maxwell says, "the walk to success must be traveled lightly."

When unforgiveness and bitterness occupy space in your heart, eventually it will show in your behavior. It will show up in the way that you treat people, how you respect them, think about them and even talk to and about them. You will find yourself treating people the way you would like to treat those who did you wrong. The sad part about it is that the people you are treating this way have nothing to do with your past. This is how good partnerships have been broken and homes have been destroyed. This is how good and godly help has been lost. All because someone didn't know how to forgive.

Stop for a moment, take a deep breath, and begin to think about who you have not yet forgiven. Is there someone in business, your family, a church member, a school classmate, or your ex-spouse, that you need to forgive? You may have to write the name(s) down. Take a moment now to do this. Be honest, don't lie to yourself.

Consider writing a letter to the person that you need to forgive, and in it tell them that you forgive them. If they are no longer living, still write the letter. Then burn it, and tell God that you forgive the person. If the person is someone that you still keep in contact with, I suggest that you call them or go see them, and forgive them. Your heart will thank you later. This will create more space in your heart, and the only thing that the heart will need to carry is love for what you're doing. A light heart travels far. A light heart produces a clean and clear mind—one that can be controlled. Such a mind includes a pure heart, and you will be a pure man or woman, because as a man thinks in his heart, so is he.

Positive Thinking is in Style

Take a minute to talk to yourself. Look in the mirror and tell yourself that you are victorious, you are a winner, you will accomplish your dreams, and you will not allow any past experience to control your future. Self talk is so important.

Exchange your negative thoughts with positive ones.

Replace, "I can't" with "I can," "I'm a loser" with "I'm a winner," and "I'm always behind" with "I am ahead." Whenever negative thoughts try to overtake you, tell them that you are being run by a new manager. Anything that tries to come into your mind but does not add value to you is not welcome. If it is not making you better, it has to go.

You have to be diligent about watching what you allow to come into your heart. Every thought must be tested. Every idea must be filtered. Your heart must be guarded, it must be

CHANGE YOUR MIND, CHANGE YOUR WALK

protected. Your heart cannot protect itself. Physically, it depends on the rib cage for protection. Emotionally, you must protect it. The Bible has some things to say about your heart. Proverbs 4:23 (NIV) says, "Above all else, guard your heart, for everything you do flows from it." Everything flows from your heart and that's the reason you must protect it. Another version translates this verse more clearly. The Easy-to-Read Version says, "Above all, be careful what you think because your thoughts control your life."

Isn't this amazing? The Bible is showing us what I like to call a water filtration system. The purpose of this system is to clean the water, to take out any toxic chemicals or bacteria that can harm the body. The filtration system will take out what doesn't belong in the water, leaving only clean, good nutrients behind. This is exactly how our filtration system ought to operate. It should process and test all of our thoughts. Once they've been tested, if it is determined that any thoughts could harm your family or your future, you must take them captive to the obedience of Christ. Here are some questions to include in your daily thought filtration process:

- Is this thought going to add value to me, my family, and my future?
- Is this thought negative? Is it trying to stop me from doing what I want to do? Is it telling me all of the possible ways that I'm going to fail?
- Will this thought promote talking badly about someone? Is it making me have a predetermined mindset toward someone?

+ Am I cheating on my spouse with this thought? Jesus said that even thinking about laying with another person's spouse is like committing adultery. And if you are willing to cheat on your spouse, you can cheat on your dreams, business, job, career, and friends.

Protect your mind. Ask yourself these questions before allowing thoughts to enter. Have this set of questions ready at all times, add to them. Remember the core principles and values that make up your filter. Whatever you value, you'll respect, and whatever you respect, you'll protect.

Whatever you value, you will respect and whatever you respect, you will protect.

Control What You Focus On

Dr. John C. Maxwell, on *The John Maxwell Leadership Podcast*, has a two-part series called "Focused Thinking." In this series he says to "stay with your thoughts long enough," to "think your ideas through." There is truth to what Dr. Maxwell is saying. What we focus on and the amount of time we take to focus on it, will determine our outcome.

Some people are daredevils, they'll try anything. They dare to push the limits. Even though you need to be willing to take some risks in life, and there are some things that you just need to go for, when it comes to ideas you must stop and think things through. This is the reason some people have good ideas but bad

44

outcomes. They didn't take into consideration the benefits of focused thinking. Focused thinking is about staying with a thought long enough to analyze it and make it better.

There are many good ideas that go nowhere because of a lack of focused thinking. When you have a good idea, make sure that you have spent the proper amount of time on it. This practice will prevent frustration and failures. After listening to coaches, mentors, podcasts and reading about this topic, I've developed a process to help you with thinking in a more focused way.

- ◆ *Think about the possibilities of your ideas.* Don't think about how the idea can go wrong. Plan, so that if and when things go wrong you will know what to do. But also focus on the positive outcome of your idea. Remember, your focus will become your outcome.
- ◆ *Share your ideas with other "possibility thinkers."* First, make sure that you can trust the people that you are going to share your idea with. Next, make sure that they are a "possibility thinker" and not a negative thinker.
- ◆ *Give other possibility thinkers permission to speak into your idea.* Many people believe that their ideas don't need any adjustments. They feel that their ideas are better than anyone else's and that it's best to not share it with others. Consider that when you allow people to speak into your ideas, you may end up with even greater ones. Others will see things that you have not been able to see because you are looking from the inside out, while they are looking from the outside in.

♦ *Revise your idea after you receive feedback.* Be sure to spend a proper amount of time thinking, talking about and listening to others' thoughts about how your idea can be achieved. Well thought out ideas will have a better return than those that are rapidly executed. Usually, when an idea is implemented too quickly, shortcuts have to be made. This can be the very reason many ideas die prematurely.

Plan and work leads to prosperity, shortcuts lead to poverty.
— *Proverbs 21:5 (NLT)*

Controlling your mind also has to do with *what* you can control. This is where many people make their biggest mistake. In business it has been said that leaders should "develop your strengths and hire your weaknesses." In other words, focus on your strengths not your weaknesses.

Entrepreneur, investor, author and philanthropist, David Nilssen, wrote an article called, "Build Your Business on Your Strengths, Hire Your Team to Cover Your Weaknesses." He says that many of the big organizations that we now know to be successful were able to get to where they are because the founder built their business on their strengths. When you work from your strengths you will love what you do, because your focus will be on the areas you enjoy. Your team will take care of areas that you're not so good at. This is a leadership principle. When you hire people that are better than you in some areas, that doesn't take power away from you. It actually makes you better.

The mistake many people make is to try to convert an area of weakness in their life into an area of strength. Most of the time, improving a weakness is beyond your control and not the best use of time. You may ask, what if my area of weakness is affecting my life, ministry, business, and family? In that case you need to call it what it is—a bad habit. The way that you overcome that is by focusing on the opposite of what you are doing. In other words, don't focus on what you don't want to be, focus on who you want to become. If you don't like to lie, don't focus on "not lying," focus on telling the truth. If you don't want to cheat on your spouse, focus on being faithful. Don't focus on not cheating. If you don't want to lose your credibility, focus on your integrity.

You Will Become What You Focus On

In my short time in ministry, I have sat in rooms with many people seeking healing, and the narrative is the same. If a man comes from an abusive father whom he hated, and he has lived his life without forgiving his father, he now confesses to me, "Pastor, I have become the guy that I hated the most, and I hate that about myself." It's the same with irresponsible mothers, drug addicted parents, and cheating spouses. The stories are all the same. People will end up confessing the phrase, "I have become the person I hated."

This happened because they focused on the negativity, the areas they hated the most in those people. When you focus on what you hate in a person it will constantly take you back to

47

unforgiveness. Your focus on negative things will cause unforgiveness to grow. Get help with forgiveness. Take the proper time to heal and focus on becoming the best version of yourself.

Chapter Review

- ◆ What exercises can you do to begin soul searching?
- ◆ Is unforgiveness stunting your growth?
- ◆ What things must you filter out of your life in order to grow?

A "No More" Mentality

Have you ever said that you would try something new and end up not doing it? I have many, many times. Let me tell you, there is something about trying that triggers a signal in your brain that you don't have to accomplish it, because "at least you tried." You don't have to give your best, because you made an attempt.

Every year, our church hosts a conference for pastors called Jumpstart. For many years my responsibility has been to serve as the driver for guest speakers. I pick them up from the airport and transport them to the church and their hotel. One year I had the honor of driving a highly honored, world-reknowned professional athlete. If I mentioned his name here you would know who he is. I, along with my friend Jonathan, served as his host for the few days he was in our city. During one of the car rides, we began to talk about life and I have never forgotten what our guest shared. He was talking to Jonathan, who said that he was going to try to do something. I don't remember exactly what he was referring to, as I was busy fighting the Chicago traffic. But our guest's reply was what caught my attention. "You know, I never say that I will try something," he said. "Trying is nothing but an excuse."

When you think about it, isn't that the truth? Anytime you say that I'm going to try something, you are automatically giving yourself permission to give up at some point. It's easy for you to come back to the biggest excuse that we all have used, "well, at least I tried." I'd like to give you a different message. Don't try it, do it. When you try, you're giving yourself permission to fail. You need to adopt a "no more" mentality. This means that you no longer accept the status quo or the same things. You no longer accept the same mediocrity, the same failures, the same mistakes, the same result, or the same low self-esteem. "No more" means that you refuse to continue in victimized thinking, negativity, or blaming others. Anything that keeps you in the same place without the opportunity to change for the better is what you have to refuse. Enough is enough.

After the pandemic hit, I made the decision that I would not fail anymore. I was sitting in my kitchen enjoying a morning cup of coffee and told my wife, "Babe, from now on this will be a year of results. We will live our lives full of seeing things completed." I'd decided that we'd no longer tolerate thinking about what could've happened or trying to see if something would work. At that moment I made the decision that anything that could be done would be done. Doing requires taking action, not making excuses. Commit to yourself that you will not *try* what you *can* do. NBA legend Michael Jordan said, "I only win and learn. I never lose." That is a perfect example of a "no more" mentality.

I have to be transparent with you. For a long time I hesitated to start writing this book. There were numerous reasons why I had a hard time, but the number one reason is that I doubted myself. Since the book was going to be motivational and inspirational, I continuously asked myself what have I accomplished that would be helpful to share with others? I don't have any success stories to show that the counsel I am sharing really works. I have failed in many things. I am not a business owner, I am not a millionaire. I am not famous, and I have not written a best selling book. I don't have a mega church. I have been pastoring in the same church for the past five years, and right before COVID hit I felt like 2020 was the year where momentum was going to increase. We had more than 500 people attending our services and then COVID came and stopped what we were gaining. I also feared my past. When people read my story and see that I even failed my wife, what would they think of me? What explanation would I have to fall back on? How would I respond to questions? When people look me up and see that I am really a nobody, what then?

Those thoughts haunted me and, for a season, stopped me from writing. I remained stuck in that place until one day I had a "no more" mentality moment. I thought, "A best seller wasn't a best seller when they wrote their book," "a successful business owner wasn't successful in the planning stages." Although planning is a very important part of building, you need to execute, too. A pastor of a mega church isn't successful in his first year pastoring. Successful people have something in common—they stopped trying and began doing. They took action.

This realization released me and I gave myself permission to write. I became even more determined to go after my goals. I abandoned the mentality that I don't have enough to give because I hadn't *yet* accomplished anything significant. That word—yet—became key. I began adding it to my thoughts. I haven't written a bestseller *yet*. I don't have a mega church *yet*. I don't have a successful business *yet*. My story hasn't become successful *yet*. Through this experience I learned something. I am willing to lead in the hardest moments. I will not hide, I will shine. That's the frame of mind that I now maintain. Some people don't like it and some have embraced it. But I changed how I think for me, not for them. I changed my mentality for my family not for other people.

I urge you to do the same. If, for whatever reason, you have allowed thoughts to haunt you and convince you that you shouldn't try, if you have "tried" things instead of "doing" things, it's time to shift. You can no longer think you don't have anything to give, that you can't offer anything of value, or that you haven't accomplished anything that people can learn from. It's time to do away with that thinking. It's time to change; make a switch. Adopt a "no more" mentality. Doing this requires you to decide that you will lead the most difficult person in the world, which is yourself. You can't hide from him or her, you can't ignore their phone calls. You can't even block their number. The person within you needs to be led, not ignored.

Here are four commitments that you can make to lead yourself to a changed mind.

1. *No More Trying.* Trying gives you permission to quit. As a matter of fact, go to the dictionary and look up the word "try" or "trying," and the word "quit." Cross them out (or

pretend to if you are using a digital version). Eliminate these words from your vocabulary. You have to make the decision that you will not try any longer. Go and do what you were born to do. Reach your maximum potential and don't allow your trying to hinder your reach. This trying mentality must be flushed out of your mind.

Don't allow your trying to hinder your reach.

---

2. *No More Failures.* I'm not saying that you'll never fail, but there is another way of seeing failures. Failures will teach you a lot, so make sure that you learn from them. Instead of throwing a pity party, ask yourself, *what can I learn from this situation?* If you allow it, every failure supplies knowledge. Every failure adds value; there is wisdom that comes from the lesson.
    We have a saying at my church, "if you're going to fail, fail fast." We have noticed through experience that sometimes people have done the same things over and over, without seeing the desired results. By the time we notice a negative pattern, so much time, effort and money has been invested that it becomes harder to pull out of a project. In other words we didn't fail fast.

What people call failure, you will call lessons.

---

3. *No More Excuses.* As I have mentioned previously, excuses are simply a reason to quit. When you look for excuses, you will find out that you are really looking for a reason to justify why you should quit. You are giving yourself permission to stop, to not continue any longer. By doing that you are accepting the belief that it is okay to be average. If being average doesn't bother you, that's fine. This part of the chapter may not be for you. But for everyone else, pay close attention.

   Personally, I don't want to be an average person and I don't think there is anything wrong with that. I don't want to look or act like everyone else. I want to be the best version of me. Being average puts me at the same level as everyone else and that is a dangerous place to be. It gives me the excuse that if I don't accomplish my potential, it's okay. Not wanting to be average means that you are willing to separate yourself from the crowd with negative voices that constantly tell you certain things cannot be done. Stop giving yourself excuses and permission to not go after what you were created to do. Put every excuse in the background and move forward.

   Cancel a mentality of excuses. From now on, do not accept any excuses in your life. Enough is enough. You were destined and called to achieve greater things. Stop being your own worst enemy. Begin to lead yourself to success.

4. *Evaluate Your Success.* Make sure that you evaluate your success and accomplishments. There are many factors

affecting why you should keep going or why you should abort a project. You may stay in it if you see some type of growth despite market conditions. But if the economy is good and what you're doing is not working, put it on hold. It may be your dream, but take a step back and learn from it. Here are five points of evaluation that I have implemented at my church:

+ Find. Look for what is working in your endeavor, and what is not working.

+ Learn. Stop doing something the same way when you keep failing at it. Learn from your mistakes and go a different way.

+ Take Notes. Write down what you've done previously and identify what can be done better.

+ Apply. The next time that you execute, use what you've taken from the previous three steps.

+ Repeat. Do all of the previous steps over again. You'll find that the way you plan and execute projects will be improved.

Five Points of Evaluation: Serving Our Community in Crisis

During the pandemic our church began giving groceries to members of our congregation and the community. We expanded from feeding fifteen families to 125 every Saturday. As the weeks went on, I noticed that only a few families that attended our grocery events lived within blocks of the church; the rest were driving from the West Side. On some Saturdays we had a lot of food left over. Even though I would save it and give it away to our church families after the Sunday services, I really wanted to give it all away on Saturdays and enlarge our reach. I started walking the blocks surrounding the church and told everyone that I saw—walking, working on their yard or even parked in cars—that we had food to give out. I then evaluated the needs of the community around the church and found out groceries were not important. The cost of real estate in the community had gone up; that part of the neighborhood was experiencing a boom. For example, a lot that cost $150,000 ten years prior was now double the price. That told me that, while well intended, my outreach wasn't for this community.

I took my five points of evaluation and did some homework on one of the communities right next to the one where our church is located. According to data from the City of Chicago, from 2014-2018 that community had 23,489 residents, of which 19,619 were Latino or Hispanic in low income housing. Of the Latino citizens, 16,355 claimed Spanish as their first language. Doing this research was important, because ours is the only campus in the New Life Covenant Church family that is completely Spanish-speaking. Although we have started a bilingual service due to changing community demographics, 99.9 percent of the people that attend speak Spanish.

One week we received a large truckload of food, so I packed up one of our shuttle buses to provide supplies for 400 families, and headed west to the community I'd researched. We had four times the amount of food we usually give away on Saturdays. I parked the bus on a major, busy street. What would usually take two hours to serve 125 families only took thirty minutes to serve 400. At the end we had no food left over. Now we have a food drive every Saturday in both locations. By taking the step to evaluate whom we were serving, we are now giving away about five times the amount of food since we started. Our reach expanded significantly and people received greatly needed help because of simple due diligence.

We found out what was working and what wasn't. We learned that our style of ministry was more critical in the other community. We took note of what we learned, and applied the changes. Now we are repeating the process.

Chapter Review

- In what areas have I given myself permission to quit?
- How can I counteract that practice?
- Evaluate your success. What can you do better? What can stay the same?
- Take a moment to study your failures. What have you learned from them? If you haven't learned anything yet, what can you learn?

SHIFT 5

Align Your Vocabulary
With Your Mindset

My dad would always tell me, "Son, many people think with their mouths." He meant that some people simply don't have a filter. They say what they think without giving it another thought. Many people don't realize the power that their words carry. Your words will produce your results.

The negative way many of us talk will only create a negative way of living. We say things based on how we feel in the moment. For example, if we make a mistake we might say things like, "I'm a loser," "Nothing good happens to me," "I will never amount to anything," "I can't overcome this depression," or "I will never survive this illness." This is low-level vocabulary and it can produce frustration, along with a lack of belief and unfulfilled potential. As a result, you will constantly go back to what is known to you—old patterns, behaviors and ways of thinking—rather than the unknown. You will find yourself stuck, unproductive and unaccomplished.

In Proverbs 18:21 (NLT) we find one of the most powerful verses in the Bible about words. It says, "The tongue can bring death or life; those who love to talk will reap the consequences."

King Solomon, the wisest and richest man that ever lived, was warning us that using the wrong vocabulary has consequences. Your way of speaking will determine what you receive. If you constantly say that your business is failing, your marriage is over, or that you are dying from an illness, that's what you're going to experience.

Changing this pattern is possible, but you have to change what you say. And that starts with your mind. Instead of just saying what you think, allow your mind to control your vocabulary. Don't say that you "can't" do something without first taking action. If you take courage and begin to speak life into your situations, if you see the possibilities of reconstruction, rebuilding and regaining momentum, you will eventually align your words with your mindset. That, my friend, is guaranteed success. This does not mean that you will ignore the storms in your life, or that you're not going to feel pain if things don't go according to plan. If there is a storm in your marriage, are you simply going to say, "Well, I'm going to believe that things are good"? The Bible talks about speaking things that are not as though they were, but often you also need to take some action to see them happen.

Don't ignore reality, just refuse to accept it. If there is a storm in your business, find a consultant to help. If there are marital issues at home, find a counselor. You must confront and tackle opposition. You must find a solution. But your outcome ultimately is determined by your words. The way that you speak going into a difficult situation will determine your coming out.

About a year ago, a member of my church, and close friend, moved to Florida. Weeks after relocating we received the terrible news that he, and his family all tested positive for COVID-19. Unfortunately he was the most affected and spent twenty-one days in the hospital. The doctor told him to sign consent papers for terminal care and to get his will ready. They called his wife many times asking her to sign the papers as well. Surprisingly the couple said the same thing, "No." The doctors tried convincing him to accept reality, that they had done everything they could for him and things were not looking good. At points during his illness he was unresponsive. But once he regained the ability to understand what was happening, he told the doctors, with his voice wavering but firm in faith, "The same way I came into this hospital is the same way I will be leaving." He continued to declare, "You're not taking me out of here in a box. I'm walking out."

Standing in Faith and Boldness

Fortunately, the doctors were wrong. They had never treated a person who was so filled with faith. After three weeks of misery, my "brother from another mother" walked out of the hospital. How could this be possible? Many other people in the same condition did not make it, yet he did. My friend, though he was literally dying spoke in such a way to refuse the doctor's prognosis. They'd done everything in their power to heal him, but he had faith in God the Healer. This is true faith. And this kind of faith will make you say things that the world cannot comprehend. He stood firm, held fast to his belief, and aligned his vocabulary with what he believed. With this combination the math doesn't fail. The result will always be the same. You will see what you said.

Another powerful story from which we can extract great teaching in this area is the story of the valley of dry bones. In Ezekiel 37, God takes the prophet in a vision to a valley of dry bones. God asks him, "Will these bones live?"

The prophet replied with what I think is the best answer I could have come up with, had I been in his shoes. "Only you know that God."

But then God gives the prophet an order, "Speak to the dry bones, and they will live." God was telling the prophet, "Of course I know. I am God. I know they will live. But I need *you* to speak to these dry bones, and then I will make them come back to life. Your job is to speak, I'll take care of the rest." In this vision the prophet spoke to the dry bones and they became a mighty army. We can apply the principle from this teaching to any situation. God knows that He can restore your marriage, grow your business, and give life to your dead dreams. But He wants you to join Him in the process. Speak to those dead things around you, and watch God bring them back to life.

Stop Complaining

My wife and kids will tell you that I can't stand complaining. I always tell them to not complain. I tend to have issues with complainers; the Lord is still dealing with me in that so please don't judge me. I'm not perfect. As a pastor I have to deal with everyone. Just because I dislike a behavior in someone, that doesn't give me the right to reject them. I must work with them. But some people complain so much that I don't want to hear from them anymore. I just want to avoid them altogether. That's why I do my best to not be a complainer. I don't bring complaints to my superiors; I bring solutions.

I recently learned something while listening to one of John Maxwell's podcasts. It was so good that we have made it part of our church culture. If someone finds a problem in the church, in our operations, our leadership, or any other area, they don't have the freedom to bring those problems to me. Many people have the magnificent ability to find problems. But to continue moving forward we need problem solvers, not problem finders. So we started this new approach that I learned from the podcast: if someone finds a problem, before they bring it to me or the leadership, they need to think about it and identify two to three possible solutions. While we are not opposed to people finding gaps or weaknesses in the way that we operate, we press them to help us problem solve.

Since we started using this new rule, it seems like problems have gone away. No one finds problems anymore. Does that mean that we really don't have any areas to improve upon? Absolutely not. We still have a lot of learning and growing to do. But this rule stopped complainers in their tracks. Now, instead of just being negative they have to work. Finding a problem is easy, but thinking of a solution for that problem is not. And everyone is not willing to put the time and effort into problem solving.

Pastor Choco has a saying, "With revelation comes responsibility." He has shared this with his staff many times. He says, "If God reveals a problem to you, is your responsibility to respond."

That same principle is what I have applied in our team. If you see a problem it is possible that God is revealing it to you, not just so that you can talk, but to do something about it. This mentality only applies to those who really want to be involved in our team. I don't allow anymore complainers on our team who have the power to speak, but don't put action behind it.

Reformed Complainers

Someone who tends to complain can change. As with everything we've been discussing in this book so far, it begins with changing their mindset. The best way to keep the mind from complaining is to always be engaged in good deeds. Serving and doing good for others makes sure that your mind is always thinking about things that are useful, positive and valuable. It keeps your mind occupied with positive thoughts.

Another way to get rid of complaining is to replace it with a thankfulness. There is beauty inside a of thankful person that creates room for their success. When you are thankful and grateful, you will attract people that will be willing to help you. People will be more prone to share their connections with you. No one wants to help a complainer, because at the end of the day, it doesn't matter how much you help them, it's never enough. Look at the people of Israel in the Old Testament. Due to their constant complaining they spent forty years in the desert. They were going in circles in the same place the entire time. Show me the place you're circling around and I will show you what type of vocabulary you have. You were not created to move in circles, you were created to go up and out.

I challenge you today to read the Bible, regardless of your background, religion or beliefs. A good book to start with is Proverbs. It will add wisdom, positivity and great life lessons to your life. It will help you to change what you say.

A Mother's Plea

At most churches, pastors occasionally invite special guests to speak to their congregations. In a particular church, the pastor would do this, and each time a certain woman would approach the speaker saying, "Preacher man, preacher man, would you pray for my daughter? She is a prostitute and she sells her body so she can support her addiction." Now, you can imagine the look in this woman's eyes; she was tearful and desperate. Every preacher would stop what they were doing and immediately, full of compassion, begin to pray for her. At times they would cry with her. I can only imagine the amount of pain that she was in. Well, this woman would do the same thing after every special event. She would ask the visiting preacher to pray for her daughter.

One day, a preacher was visitng the church, and after the service she went to him and made her desperate plea, "Preacher man, preacher man, would you pray for my daughter? She is a prostitute and she sells her body so she can support her addiction." But this time, to her surprise, this preacher looked at her and said, "As long as you continue to confess that she is a prostitute that's all she will ever be. You need to speak what you want her to be not what she is." He prayed for the woman, "God help this woman align her words with your will, in the name of Jesus. Amen." When he finished praying, he turned and walked away.

The woman was shocked and wondered what had just happened. She began to think about what the preacher had said to her. The next morning when she saw her daughter in the corner, she greeted her, "Hi baby, I hope that you're doing well. I want you to know that you are a missionary for Jesus." The daughter's friends laughed, and made fun of her. They told her that her mom had gone crazy. Embarrassed, the daughter told her mother to leave. But every time the mother saw her daughter, she spoke over her life, "You are a missionary for Jesus."

One day the mother was praying in her living room, crying out to God, "Lord, change my daughter, transform her Lord, please, I beg of you." Suddenly, she heard a knock at the door. "Come in, the door is open," she said.

The mother sat on her sofa, and wiped the tears from her eyes. She looked up and saw a skinny young woman standing in front of her. She had black marks up and down her arms due to injecting drugs into her body. The mother realized it was her daughter.

"Mom," the daughter said.

The mother stood, "Yes, baby," she replied.

"Mom, I don't know what you have done to me, but I don't want to do drugs anymore. I don't want to sell my body anymore. I want to serve Jesus for the rest of my life." Today, this young woman is a missionary for Christ.

Speak only what you want to see, and not what you don't want to see. Align your words with your mindset.

Chapter Review

- ♦ Proverbs 18:21 reminds us about the power of our tongue. How must you change your vocabulary in order to succeed?
- ♦ Where has God revealed gaps in your life?
- ♦ Using faith and boldness, how would you address them?

SHIFT 6

Your Gifts to God

Last summer, two associate pastors from my campus, Pastors Victor Santiago, whom I mentioned earlier, and Victor Martinez, and I had just completed a discipleship session conducted live on social media. At the end of the study, I stayed on for a few minutes to talk to the pastors. I asked them to keep me in their prayers as I worked on writing this book. It was my first time sharing this with them. No one from my church knew at the time that I was writing a book. They were the first ones I told. They were so happy for me. We had a good conversation and I left the call feeling excited.

I encourage you to find pastors, business owners, entrepreneurs and leaders to be part of your life, who will celebrate your victories. It is so important to surround yourself with these kinds of people. They have the ability to feel proud of your accomplishments and are excited to celebrate with you. They are not jealous of you and want the best for you.

Pastor Martinez said, "Pastor, I had never spoken to you in this way but I'm going to dare to tell you this. I am happy for you, but Pastor..." he continued with his calm way of speaking. "The book is already done, all you have to do is write it. It's in you, all you have to do is release it. Let it out."

I was wowed by what he said. *It's already in you...* I thanked him for being candid with me and said, "Thank you. You just confirmed the title for one of the chapters of the book: *Your Accomplishments are Your Gifts to God.*

Delight in the Lord

Psalm 37:4 (NIV) says, "Take delight in the Lord, and he will give you the desires of your heart." Albert Barnes Notes on the Whole Bible gives a good explanation of the word delight, "to find delight or pleasure in anything. The meaning here is that we should seek our happiness in God—in His being, His perfections, His friendship and His love." Our happiness should be in our Creator. When we delight in Him, and all of His characteristics what happens is the next part of this verse that says: "He will give you the desires of your heart."

This verse is not saying that God will give you anything that you ask or think. This is not the Bruce Almighty movie, where the famous actor Jim Carrey gets the power to be God and answers 'yes' to all of the prayers in one night. Because if that were true, there would be a lot of prayers that should've been answered already. What the verse is actually saying is that when we delight in God, He will give you what you desire. One way to understand the last part of that verse is that "God will place dreams and desires in your heart." So when you delight in Him, when you find happiness in Him, when you find joy in His friendship and love, you will desire what He wants for you. God will place the dream in your heart, but it is your job to make it a reality.

Make it Happen

Pastor Choco served as the senior pastor of our church for almost twenty years, before he became the general treasurer of the Assemblies of God, which is the denomination our church is under. The church began to have success under his leadership and became known for our outreach ministry, and how we serve the community. Pastors from other churches in the area were visiting our church and calling to learn what we were doing that was working so well.

While in flight for a mission trip in Camden, NJ, Pastor Choco and Pastor Rico, an executive pastor at the church, were seated next to each other on the plane. Pastor Choco told Pastor Rico, "I feel in my heart that the Lord is leading me to put something together that will help pastors come to Chicago, learn what we are doing, take it to their church, and apply it." As he talked, he grabbed a napkin and began to draw and write out his vision for a conference.

"I want to create an experience in the form of a conference for pastors and leaders to come from all over the nation and see with their own eyes what the Lord is doing with us. Let's call it "Jumpstart," because many pastors and leaders need a jumpstart in their ministries, lives, families and dreams. When he was finished writing, Pastor Choco handed the napkin to Pastor Rico and said, "Make it happen."

In this same way, when we delight in the Lord, it is like we are sitting next to Him in a plane called life, journeying to our final destination, which, according to what I believe, is heaven. God will hand blueprints, ideas and visions to us and say, "Make it happen." What He gives us may not look clear but it is a vision for where to go. It is a dream, a business to start, areas to change in our lives, or habits to leave behind because where you're going you need to travel light. God will drop things in your lap for you to develop.

You may be wondering if God is a Creator, why doesn't He make these things happen Himself? The only answer I have for you is that He could absolutely do it without us, but He wishes not to. He chooses to accomplish things through us, so that we can be part of His glorious work here on earth. It's like the man who had bought a land full of rocks, and had worked hard to develop the land. He built a nice garden with beautiful flowers, trees, and expertly cut grass. It was a paradise. A friend of the man went to visit him, saw the land and said to him, "Wow, what beautiful land God has given you."

The man replied, "Yeah, I know. But I wish you had seen it when it belonged to God alone."

God wants you to partner with Him to build greatness. When He gives you a dream, that's His gift to you. Making it happen is your gift to God. It is a great possibility that any dream designed to better the life of others, and even yourself, is from God. Don't be afraid to make it happen. God wouldn't have given you the gift if He didn't believe that you could make it happen.

Imagine that God looks at you and sees that what He has placed in your heart has been accomplished. It is done. Finished. How do you think that would make Him feel?

The Parable of the Talents

It is like the parable of the talents (see Matthew 25:14-30). A CEO goes away on a business trip, but before he leaves, he calls three of his employees and gives them stock. To the first employee he gives five shares of stock. To the second employee he gives two. And to the third employee he gives one.

When the CEO returned from his trip, he was pleased with the first two employees because they both had doubled their shares. The one who received five, returned five more, and the one who received two, returned two more. But when he got to the third employee, the one he gave just one share, he was not pleased. He didn't double it, or at least gain interest on it. He simply buried the stock and returned the same amount that he'd received. In this story Jesus calls the man lazy. When God gives you a dream He expects you to accomplish it, and when you do, you are honoring Him with your accomplishments. So, don't be lazy, make it happen. The easy thing to do would be to bury it. But the hard thing to do is to develop it.

There are many buried ideas and visions that never saw the light of day. Motivational speaker, Les Brown, said, "The graveyard is the richest place on earth, because it is here that you will find all the hopes and dreams that were never fulfilled, the books that were never written, the songs that were never sung, the inventions that were never shared, the cures that were never discovered, all because someone was too afraid to take that first step, keep with the problem, or determine to carry out their dream." This is powerful. Do not abandon your dream. Making it happen will bring so much joy to you and to the people around you. But most importantly, it will bring glory to God. The individuals in the Parable of the Talents multiplied what was placed in their hands. They made it a reality. Not only were they blessed, but other people benefited from their accomplishments.

How to Multiply Your Gift

When God gives you a big dream, you have to develop it, and it will likely require multiplication to become all that it is supposed to be. You will need to multiply yourself, your efforts and your talent. The way that you create multiplication is by asking for help. Create a team around your God-given dream, and add the best people to help you. This may take a mindset shift, because many people believe that to achieve anything significant they have to do it all on their own. If this is your belief, you will need to work on changing your mind. Oliver Wendell Holmes said, "A mind that is stretched by a new experience can never go back to its old dimensions."

In *The 17 Indisputable Laws of Teamwork*, John Maxwell writes about the "The Law of Significance." He says, "One is too small of a number to achieve greatness." Isn't that the truth? Whenever you want to accomplish anything big, you can't do it alone. Many times the reason is because the task is difficult. You will see it as impossible when you're viewing it alone. Former U.S. President Lyndon B. Johnson said, "There are no problems we cannot solve together, and very few that we can solve by ourselves."

When we fail to fulfill a God-given dream, we fail to accomplish a purpose in our life and in the lives of others. Imagine how many people would be blessed if you accomplished the dream that you have in your heart. What adds to the blessing is not just the accomplishment of the dream, but the process to get there. You should assess how many people were changed during the process and how much value was added to your team members. The journey is always more important and valuable than the dream itself. It is in the journey that you and your people grow. Remember, the accomplishment is not intended just to benefit you, but your team and future generations. You can only do that if you ask for help, and that can only happen with a changed mind.

When we refuse to go after a God-given dream we are closing the door on something divine to be revealed in our life and in the lives of others. God is trusting you to bring to earth something that only can happen through an accomplished dream that was placed inside of you before the beginning of time. Only your accomplished dream can open a specific door. Through your fulfilled dream, the world will see something divine on earth.

Chapter Review

- ◆ What desires are in your heart that you have not yet made a reality?
- ◆ Will they bless others more than you?
- ◆ What gifts or fulfilled dreams are you desiring to present to God?

Ignore Negativity

Negativity. This word is the opposite of positivity, but it means so much more. When I Googled "What is negativity?" I got the following definition: negativity is the expression of criticism of or pessimism about something. Criticism means the expression of disapproval, and pessimism means a tendency to see the worst aspect of things or believe that the worst will happen; a lack of hope or confidence in the future. Now, let's take a closer look at negativity overall. It is the expression of disapproval from someone who has the tendency to see the worst aspect of things, and believes that the worst will happen. They don't have hope or confidence in the future.

All of that is incorporated into negativity, and for some odd reason we tend to believe the "expression of the expression." This means that we are not even believing something first hand. We are believing something based on other information—or second hand. A negative person is one whom you're listening to that usually views things as being in the worst shape. They believe the worst will happen, everything will fail, and the cup is half empty. Because of that, they don't work to accomplish anything. If your circle of advisors is made up of people with beliefs like this, you need a serious change in counsel.

Handling Your Haters

People who are negative don't dare to go after their own dreams. Since they are scared and afraid of accomplishing their dream, they will try to talk you into abandoning yours. They will speak negatively about it and will tell you all the possible reasons why you shouldn't do it or go after it and why it wouldn't work. Look at your dreams as if they are a child that God gave you. You wouldn't abandon that child, would you? You would love them. Similarly, if God gave you a dream, you don't have the right to abandon it and people don't have the right to speak negatively about it. Ignore the naysayers long enough to achieve your goals. Your accomplishments will silence the critics.

Isn't it funny that people will try to stop you from doing something that you love because they think that they are helping you? They will start or end a conversation by saying things like: "I'm telling you this because I care," "I don't want you to fail," "I don't want you to get hurt," or "I want you to look good." I'm not saying that these people don't actually care; many of them such as parents, brothers, sisters, best friends and spouses, actually do. But what they don't realize is that their words carry weight. When they try to stop you from doing what you love, if it doesn't work all you will remember is that they didn't support you—not that they care. We should never try to pull someone away from doing something they love, as long as what they're doing is not harmful.

There is another group of people who will say negative comments about your dreams, not because they want to show you they care, but because that's all they know. They don't know how to be supportive of people, to engage with them or see them succeed. There could be many reasons why these individuals are the way that they are. One reason could be because they have been hurt by a past failure and they can't find the way to overcome that. The problem comes when they apply their mistakes to you. Critics will make false claims about you, but like Pastor Choco says, "people will feed pigeons but shoot eagles." If you feel that at some point you're getting shot at, it's just an indication that you're an eagle, soaring high.

Negative-minded people want what you have. They want your go-getter mentality, or as we've learned from the late Kobe Bryant, "the Mamba Mentality". Some people have not trained their minds to dominate in their lives. So when they see you excelling and mounting up on accomplishments, they turn into critics. They can't figure out how you made it, but trust me, they would love to know. Unfortunately, it is easier to criticize others than to ask for help.

If any of these scenarios apply to you, repent. Apologize. You should learn how to celebrate the success of others. When you learn to celebrate other people, that will position you to be next in line. If you are in the position of being criticized or having negative things said about you, you will find that those same unsupportive people will come back to you. In these moments you need to forgive and teach them about how you found success. Forgiveness is a platform of humility and God promotes the humble. There will be others who will continue to hate on you. Choose to love them anyway.

People will hate on what they don't have, and talk about what they don't understand.

The Inner Critic

There is yet another person who you may need to ignore — yourself. Anytime you begin to talk yourself out of going for your dreams, that's the moment you need to ignore your self talk. There are a couple of ways that you can do that — the first is to replace your negative thinking with positive thinking. This is more simple than what you may think. Replacing your old form of thinking basically means monitoring your thoughts, and keeping a lookout for what enters your mind.

Whenever you have a plan, an idea for your business or ministry, or a personal goal, instead of looking at what could go wrong, look at what can go right. I'm certain you have used the "what if…" excuse. What if I fail? What if I lose everything? What if this doesn't work? By asking "what if" over and over, you have allowed something that is not real to stop you. Do you realize that? The "what ifs" never seem to happen. They are not real. But you have placed value on something that has the potential to hijack your plans. You've ignored the possibilities.

To get to the possiblities, you need to change the meaning of your "what if" questions to positives. Envision yourself making your goal happen. What if you succeed? What if you win? What if this is exactly what you're supposed to do? What if the satisfaction of your accomplishments is far more gratifying than the pain of failure? Asking yourself these questions will not hold you back, instead they will motivate you to go after what you were made to do.

There is a second way that you can change your old ways of thinking—move ahead despite fear. Imagine a loved one—it could be your child, spouse, parent or grandchild—is hanging from a rope in between two skyscrapers. They are stuck due to a malfunction in the harness they are wearing. Experts won't be able to get to them before the harness breaks, but don't fear, you have in your hand the solution that can save the day. The rope can easily hold both of you, but you don't have much time to complete the rescue. In this situation, wouldn't you immediately move to do everything in your power to get to and save your loved one? Of course you would, but, why? The simple answer is love. First John 4:18 says, "There is no fear in love, but perfect love drives out fear..."

Isn't that the truth? You could be afraid, but because of love you would do everything in your power to save your loved one. People have done crazy things because of love. It will make you do some ridiculous things, and it also will give you the courage to do some things you would never otherwise do. Recently there was a story in the news about a mother in Florida who jumped into a lake to save her child from an alligator attack. I'm sure that in any other circumstance she wouldn't dare to jump in water known to be full of alligators. But since her child was in danger, she didn't hesitate to do what she had to do. Love did not allow her to think about herself; love made her think about her child.

Love puts others first. First John says it well, "There is no fear in love." But even in dangerous situations, love will be greater than fear and will drive it out. Love will make you do some things that in your rational mind doesn't make sense. What if you had superhero power, like Superman, The Incredible Hulk or Thor, and you have a lot of children. One day for some odd reason your children decide to start beating you up. Now, you are a superhero. You are used to fighting monsters, and intruders from other planets that are far stronger than your children. But because these are your children, you decide not to fight back. Why? Because you love them. You decide not to fight, because if you did, you know you would kill them. This story parallels a similar one in the Bible.

Jesus, Our Superhero

There was a man named Jesus, God's Son. He was, and is, the best superhero ever. He came to earth and died at the hand of God's creation, which actually belonged to Him. They fought against and eventually crucified Jesus, and He had the power to destroy them all. He had the power to come down from the cross, but decided not to because He loved them. Jesus was nailed to a cross. He was in excruciating pain, and part of Him probably wanted to rebel against God's plan and destroy them all. But He didn't do any of that. Instead He said, "Father, forgive them because they do not know what they're doing." This is an act of love. Jesus knew that if He aborted His Father's plan, the human race could not be saved, and we would not have access to heaven. That was the dream that God the Father has had for us all along. His desire is that we spend eternity with Him in heaven. To fulfill this dream, the Father gave up Jesus as a substitute for us. Jesus took our place on the cross. This is love.

Now, the Father has placed dreams in us to accomplish and we are going to let fear stop us? After seeing Jesus' example, how could we? You need to fall in love with your dreams in such a way that fear it is no longer a factor for you. Remember the television show "Fear Factor"? At the end, after the contestants overcome many obstacles, the host tells the winner, "fear is no longer a factor for you." I'll tell you the same thing. Fear can no longer be an excuse. That needs to stop today. Make a commitment right now that you will no longer listen to fear. Your own negativity may have produced it, but you can move ahead despite it.

Effects of Overcoming Negativity

I want to offer a bit of advice as I close this chapter. In your process of overcoming negativity, your courage will be tested, and your family will be tested. When you begin a journey of chasing your dreams, you need to be very clear with your spouse and family. Be honest with them, ask them to give you some time to dedicate to reaching your goal. Explain that they will notice some changes in you, and encourage them that the changes are for the better. Let them know that this journey will cost you sleep, rest and energy, but they will not be neglected. You can't afford to reach your dreams and lose your loved ones. God does not want you to neglect your family. As a man of God, I know that my wife and my kids are my first ministry.

When I go after anything in life, if it is not going to bring good to my family I don't do it. I've learned from experience.

Many times I have pursued things that caused me to neglect my family. Now I know to bow out once I see trouble on the horizon. And for me, trouble is neglecting my family. My wife and I have agreed that before I begin a new project, I talk to her and we come up with a plan so I can accomplish the assignment without impacting my home. You might consider doing the same thing. But when you start, ask yourself "How will this benefit me and my family"? If you can't answer that question that's a sign you need to let it go.

Chapter Review

- How does negativity show up in your life?
- How do you handle it?
- Knowing that we can be our own worst critic, how can you avoid negative self-talk?
- Why are these questions are important to answer?

SHIFT 8

Just Go

Our church runs a school of ministry where people go deeper into the word of God, prepare to serve, and are trained to serve in leadership and pastoral service. One night after class—I was enrolled as a student at the time—I was talking to a young woman in the parking lot. She was telling me about some things she wanted to initiate, but she didn't know how to get started. I told her that she had a good plan, and explored with her how she could possibly begin, but still whe didn't know how or didn't want to get started.

"When you are about to leave your house to go to your job in the morning, do you wait for every traffic light to be green before leaving?" I asked.

"No," she said. "That would be crazy."

"Right," I responded. "In life it's similar. When you're going after your dreams you can't wait for circumstances to be perfect, you just move. When you come to a red light, you simply stop and wait, because you know that you'll soon be cleared to pass. The light will change soon. I ended the conversation by telling her: "just go."

Procrastination is the enemy of success.

Many people find themselves in similar situations. They wait for the perfect scenario, opportunity, storm or for all of the traffic lights to be green before they go. If that's you, allow me to bring you back to reality. What you are doing is not called waiting—it's called procrastination, and as long as you continue to practice this, you will die with your dreams still inside of you. I urge you to stop procrastinating on things that need action.

Procrastination is a bad habit that needs to be destroyed in order for you to find success. Procrastination is not of God. The word "go" appears in Scripture 1,542 times. The word "stay" appears sixty-two times. You do the math. It seems like God wants you to "go" forward. This word implies movement of all kinds. But the meaning of this word is powerful. In the Old Testament the words used for "to go," are *halakh* and *yalakh*. Both words, in their original sense, mean "to walk." Since the title of this book is *Shift! Change Your Mind, Change Your Walk*, essentially what we are saying is, if you change your mind you will change your "go," or your direction.

Keep Moving

There are many stories in the Bible where God told people to go:

"Abram, go to a place I will show you."
"Moses 'go' return to Egypt."
"Joshua, tell my people to march (to go) around the city."

"Paul, go to the city."

"Disciples, 'go' to Jerusalem and stay.

I hope you see my point. God wants us to be on the move, to walk forward. It is in movement that things get accomplished. Moving is a sign of life. If you're a parent you will relate to this. I remember when my daughter was born. When we brought her home from the hospital, I would go to the crib to check on her. I stared at her until I saw her little belly moving up and down, with each breath. Movement is a sign of life.

If you want to give life to your dreams, start moving. There is no better time in history where movement will be more appreciated than now. In a culture and season where words such as, "the new normal," "social distancing," "quarantine," and many others have stopped us, movement is needed. We need to move towards our dreams, goals, and new horizons. People are in need of inspiration and leadership. They are looking for someone to start moving so that they can follow. So, when are you going to start moving? I'm here to tell you that the time is now. Just go.

Many people have allowed procrastination to keep them in the same place. So, I want to give you three important words that will kill the procrastination in you.

Commitment

The first thing that you need to do to overcome procrastination is commit to your dreams. Stay committed to your goals. Think about what you want to accomplish or develop. Whatever it is, you need to be committed to it.

Commitment will help you hold your ground when storms come. It will keep you firm. Talk to couples that have been married for over thirty years. Ask them what has been their secret. Ask them if they felt in love with their spouse for the entire thirty years of marriage. I would almost guarantee all of them would say no. Long term love is not based on a feeling, it comes from commitment. With your goals and dreams, it is the same way. You are not going to feel in love every step of the way.

85

But if you stay committed, you will not quit. Winners never quit and quitters never win. Winners are committed and quitters are not. It is as simple as that.

I recommend writing out your commitments. Specifically, write down why you need to stay committed. What does the dream or goal means to you? Why is it so important for you to accomplish? Trust me, your why will give you the reason to commit. Your why will keep you pushing forward in moments when the feeling to quit comes. Because those moments *will* come. Anytime you want to accomplish something that is valuable, that you love, and it has the potential to bless and change your life and that of others, you will see opposition like never before.

The feeling of quitting during a challenging time is inevitable. Your thoughts will begin to play tricks on you. You'll think things like, "You're not cut out for this," "This is too hard," "It is too much," "I'm not going to be able to do this," "There is no shame in quitting," and so on. But it is in those moments that commitment kicks in. Commitment shines in the face of opposition. In the midst of opposition your commitment will keep you firm on your journey towards your dreams, and your eyes fixed on the prize. On the other side of opposition you will find that you have accomplished your dreams. Your commitment kept you going. Just like a husband who stays committed to his wife even in the moments where he does not feel the same type of love for her, he is reminded of the vows he made in front of God, "'til death do us part." Commitment, my friend, will keep you in the game.

After writing down your commitment, sign and date it, and post it in a place where you will see it often. Read it aloud daily. Constantly go back to it. This will keep your "why"—the reason you are making the commitment in the first place—in front of you all of the time. Your commitment will keep you in the right place, even if you don't want to be there. But because you gave your word, you stayed, and you have to value what you said. Nowadays, though, it seems like words don't have the same value. As a young man, I remember seeing my dad making a

CHANGE YOUR MIND, CHANGE YOUR WALK

business transaction with words, and the signature was a handshake. Those were the days. There was no paperwork, a person's word was it. To be honest I remember longing to experience that. Where I would make an agreement and shake peoples' hands, and that would be enough. Unfortunately it is not that way anymore. I'm not saying that contracts are not valid. We need them so that people do not take advantage of us. What I'm saying is that it seems as if we don't value words like we used to. People don't seem to be committed to their words like before, but we should. Value your words, they are your best representative, and honor your commitments. You will find that your commitment kills procrastination.

One action that I have taken that has helped me in keeping my commitments is going to people that I highly respect and telling them about my goals. Those people hold me accountable for my words. Also, the fact that I shared them with those people puts pressure on me to make those things a reality. It pushes me to work hard on my goals, because if not I will look like that guy that talks a lot, but has no action. I recommend you do the same. If you want to up your level of commitment, go to people whom you admire and tell them about your dreams. That conversation, along with your written "why", will keep you focused and it will maintain your commitment to work hard even in moments where you don't feel like it. Trust me, a little pressure is needed to reach your best.

Keep Moving

Movement is the enemy of procrastination. Pastor Choco says, "the devil can't hit a moving target." Life will try to hit you, and the enemy of your dreams will try to destroy them even before you start. But if you keep moving, they can't get to you.

I grew up in the Spanish Pentecostal Church of God International Movement and my father was a pastor in the organization. I became a leader in my youth, and began to excel in an organization called AJEC, as part of the Midwest Region in the U.S. We had local church, district and regional leaders. First I was the youth leader at my local church. Then I became the youth leader of my district in Chicago. At the age of twenty-one I became the youngest Regional Youth Leader of the organization. I was a twenty-one year old young man covering ten states—an entire region of the nation. I know that was God's doing.

One of the responsibilities of my position was to work with a team to host an annual youth convention. The way it worked in the past is that a church from our region would host the convention. They would take on the financial burden and receive the profits as well. One year, I don't know how, but I convinced an entire region that we would do what we had never done before. As a youth organization with little to no money in the bank, we would host the following year's convention.

Many people said I was crazy. But I did what any leader would do, I built an entire team around a vision. I began to assign projects to people, so everyone had a different task. My job was to find the facilities and the speakers for the conference. During the planning process, I almost called my regional president of the pastors, who also was my superior and to whom I reported, to tell him that we couldn't do it. But, my dream and desire were bigger than the feeling of failure. As a result, a group of young people accomplished what had never been done before in our region. We hosted our youth convention without having financial support from a local church. It was a huge achievment that people still talk about today; our AJEC team did an amazing job.

Through the success of that event, we set the standard and left the youth organization in good standing. We also brought along two previous regional leaders who had smilar goals, but were unable to accomplish it themselves. I invited them to serve on our advisory team so they could be a part of what we were achieving.

Advice for Leading

The prior regional leaders that I included on our team knew how to stay in their lane and allowed me to lead. I felt comfortable adding them to the group and working with them. If you're going to incorporate people who are accustomed to leading be clear on expectations in the beginning. Make sure you give them specific instructions and share your heart. Most importantly, you need to trust them.

Be Passionate

Another thing that you can do to overcome procrastination is to be passionate. Passion will keep you moving even in moments when you can't go on any longer. When you feel like giving up, passion will keep you going. Passion is the engine of movement. It will make you love your dreams and your goals so much that you will work toward them with such a high level of performance, you'll give your best.

Passion is a friend of excellence. It will make sure that everything you do is done in excellence and that, my friend, is the secret. When you care enough to give your best every time you show up to your business, your dreams, your job, your home, to serve at your local church, with an excellence mindset, that will make the difference. If you are passionate about being there, you won't lack energy. Your service will always be the best. Excellent service is what determines if a person will come to a restaurant often or once a year. Excellence is what makes the difference between someone visiting you at your church once, or staying with you when he visits.

Passion makes you move toward your dream. It's contagious. When someone serves or works with passion that trickles down to others.

"Excellence honors God and inspires others."
—Pastor Bill Hybels

If you are not passionate about your dreams you have two choices: 1. find passion in what you do and revive that passion, or

2. find something else to do. If you're not going to offer your best, why do it?

Stop for a moment and ask yourself, "Am I giving my best?" "Am I living the best version of me?" "Am I passionate about what I'm doing?" If the answer is no, my friend, you must find passion in what's in front of you or change what you are doing. Whatever you do, passion has to be part of it.

Passion was what made me keep moving during the work of the youth convention. And it is what makes me stay in ministry. Trust me, it is not the money. Lord knows that there have been times when I've thought about doing something else, but then I realize that I love what I do. So I keep doing what I love. That's passion. I've come to a point in my life where I say 'no' to things that I'm not passionate about. This is not to say that I haven't started some things that I wasn't passionate about at first, but later on I found passion in it. That can happen sometimes, but don't stay in anything for too long without passion. It will make you hate what you do and lose friendships.

I have seen it time and time again, where people will jump on something just because they don't know how to say no. The danger in that is that they may jump into a project that is being managed by a team. Without the same level of passion as everyone else, they may find that they have become a burden. There is nothing worse in a project than to have someone that doesn't want to be part of the team. Your lack of passion will show in your lack of enthusiasm. If this describes you, find passion or move out. Simply accept that it is not for you.

Chapter Review

- ◆ When thinking about success, right now, are you waiting or procrastinating?
- ◆ For a current project, in what areas do you need to move and commit?
- ◆ Thinking about how passion keeps us moving, how can you be sure to stay passionate?

SHIFT 9

Believe That You Can

A good friend of mine, Gicele Wray-Lindley, recently published her first book, a thirty-one day devotional for business owners titled, "Permission To Prosper." Many people have given themselves permission to fail instead of prospering. They constantly think that they "can't". That's why I brought up my friend's book, because I love the title. Your Creator has already given you permission to prosper. You don't need to ask, permission has been granted to you. Whether you believe in God or not, He wants you to prosper. You know, that's a principle of achievement. Believing and understanding that you can. Give yourself permission to achieve—to get up and go after what you want.

Believing: A Principle for Achievement

The Bible says, "I can do all things through Christ who gives me the strength to do it." And you have to just believe and say it to yourself, "I can." Is that hard for you to do? Is that too hard to believe? That you can? If it is, you must change your mindset, from "I can't," or "I don't know if I should," to "I can." The mindset you use when you approach your goals will determine if you will or won't achieve what you're going after. If you study the mindset of highly successful people, such as athletes, business owners, actors, inventors, innovators and the list goes on, you will find that they have a "yes, I can" mindset.

This was the very same phrase that captivated America during the 2008 election. In a nation where what was about to happen had never been done before, someone said, "yes we can." In a nation where all the odds were against a candidate, he decided to say, "yes we can." This man thought that it was time to make history in this country despite the naysaying and even the death threats he received after announcing his candidacy for president of the United States of America. He continued to say, "yes we can," throughout the entire race and as you know on November 4, 2008 he was elected as the first African American President of this great nation. I'm speaking of none other than President Barack Obama. I remember during my freshman year in high school, I asked my history teacher if we were ready to see an African American president in this country. His reply was, "Mr. Medina, someday but not today." And just ten years later "someday" became a reality—all because someone said, "yes we can."

Make "Someday" a Reality

One of the reasons people find it difficult to have a "yes I can" mindset is that they count themselves out. They say they can't do something without knowing or making things happen to improve their lives. Don't count yourself out. Don't become your biggest enemy. We have established that you need to avoid negative people, but you also need to avoid the negative inner you. Your inner negative voice can be the most destructive. It wants to rise up above your will and control your destiny. When we allow this type of mentality to dominate, we will talk ourselves out of doing the things we love to do—because we thought that we couldn't do them. Then we become frustrated with ourselves and take it out on our spouses, children, supervisors, and the world, all because we talked ourselves out of our destiny.

If this situation sounds familiar to you and you're always angry, get over yourself. Stop feeling sorry for yourself and blaming others for your lack of motivation. Stop using your past as an excuse to not have a better future. You can't change your past, but you can determine your future with your mindset and your decisions today. Change your mind today and have a better walk tomorrow.

We fear failure so much that it is unbelievable. Who cares what people might say if you fail? Who cares what they think? That doesn't matter. What matters is that if you continue regretting not going after something, you could negatively impact the relationship with your family. Your family is not at fault for your failures, you are. It became your responsibility the moment you allowed your negative thinking to control your actions. Failure is not losing your business, ideas, job, or constantly losing your battle with addiction. That's not failure, that's struggle. That's the fight of life. Failure is deciding to give up. So STOP making your loved ones pay for something they don't owe you.

CHANGE YOUR MIND, CHANGE YOUR WALK

Failure is the moment you decide to give up.

Failure begins the moment you fear it. You think about it in such a way that you believe it, so it happens. What you believe is what you receive. I'm going to let you in on a secret: *fear fears a fearless man*. When you become fearless, fear will avoid you. Don't fear failure. Fear giving up.

Most of the time we fear things that haven't even happened, simply because we thought about it. We thought about the "what ifs." Well, change that. See yourself doing it, achieving it, conquering it. Make that which was just a dream, a reality. Think about it long enough to go after it and make it happen.

See yourself coming out of addiction. Many people will constantly say things to themselves such as: I can't do it! I tried and I can't do it! I have heard this many times. As with anything in life, if you see yourself doing it in your mind you can walk it out in your flesh. But you have to believe that you can. Like we established before, "your words have to be aligned with your mindset." I read a post on Instagram that said:

"Everything in life starts with your mindset first and your actions second. Your actions follow your thoughts, your beliefs and ideas. To make a shift, to free your energy, start with getting your mind right, and then,

95

take action."

— *Silvester McNutt III*

You see, you need to see yourself doing what you want to do. Yes, you can get out of drug addiction. Yes, you can get out of pornography. Yes, you can get out of sexual immorality. Yes, you can achieve your goals. Yes, you can reach your dreams and make them a reality. Yes, you can control your thoughts. Yes, you can become the first doctor or lawyer in your family. Yes, you can become a millionaire and a billionaire. Yes, you can become the first Hispanic president of the United State of America. Yes, you can! Why not? If that's what you want, keep saying to yourself, yes I can. Yes I can!

If what you are going after has never been done before, you have the opportunity to prove that it can be done. Don't let the failures of others stop you from reaching your goals. Just because someone tried something and they didn't succeed at it, doesn't mean that it is impossible. With God everything is possible. You can! Children of God, "church folks," can sometimes be the most weak-minded people. We think we can't when God already has said to us, yes you can. You can do all things through Christ who strengthens you. Your strength comes from the Lord. You are the head and not the tail. You are more than a conqueror. All you need is to believe that you can do it and walk toward your goals, dreams, freedom, and develop that which is in you.

I read an amazing story in the book, *Move Ahead with Possibility Thinking,* by Robert H. Schuller, and it is a true example of a "yes you can" mentality. A man visits a leprosarium—a hotpital for people with leprosy—in Japan. Many of the patients had lost their eyesight and were learning to read by the Braille system. One blind leper tried to learn to read braille, only to find that the deterioration caused by the disease left his fingers so insensitive that he was unable to feel the raised lettering. He had reason to give up, but did he? No. This man had a "yes I can" mentality. Since he had trouble with his fingers, he tried using his toes. But he found that the feeling in his toes was lacking, too. What options did he have left? He remembered that he had one other sensitive part of his body that might serve him. He tried and it worked! Today, this man reads his Braille Bible—with his tongue

This story may sound unbelieveable, but it's really about determination and courage. The man had a "yes I can" mentality. This man was not willing to give up because he understood that he could do whatever he set his mind to, and you can, too. You can reach higher. You can go further. You can do all that you set your mind to do. All you have to do is *Shift!* and *Change Your Mind* to *Change Your Walk.*

Chapter Review

+ Why is it so hard to believe in yourself?
+ If there's one thing to fear, it is fear itself. How can you stay on the right track and maintain control of your thoughts?

A NEW WALK

This book was written around my experiences of having faith in God, but I promise you that it has not been my intention to impose my faith on you. I wrote it in this way because God has been so good to me that I want to share Him with everyone I can. If you are not a believer in God and His Son Jesus, and you want to know Jesus and begin a personal relationship with Him, I invite you to make this prayer with me:

> "Lord Jesus, come into my heart. Forgive me of my sins. I accept you as my Lord and Savior. Write my name in the book of life and by faith I believe I am a new person. In Jesus' name, amen."

If you recited this statement then you are now part of God's family; welcome! For more information to help guide you in your new walk with Jesus, I invite you to find a local church near you, visit and grow there.

NOTES

1. Robert H. Schuller, "Move Ahead With Possibility Thinking," (Jove. 1986), pages 55-69.

2. Psalm 37 www.biblehub.com, Accessed 2020, https://biblehub.com/commentaries/barnes/psalms/37.htm[1]

Made in the USA
Middletown, DE
14 June 2022